eco ella

A PAPER DOLL BOOK

Reuse

Recycle

Reduce

STORY and ILLUSTRATION by KIRSTEN BENEKE

Eco Ella
A Paper Doll Book
© 2009 by Kristen Beneke

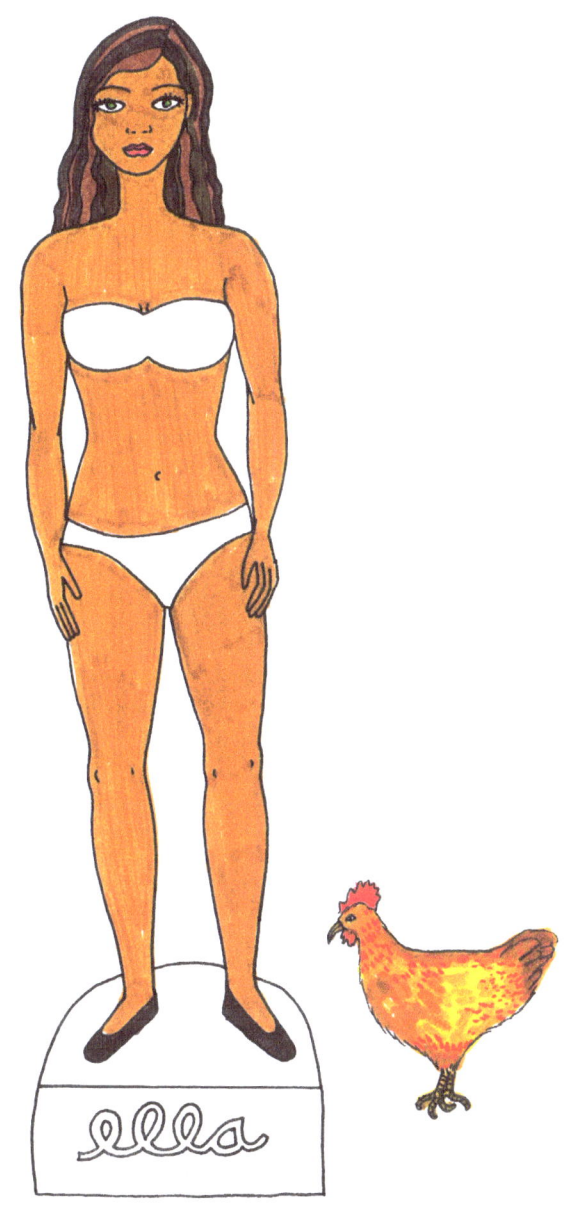

Ella believed deep in her heart, if everyone who had the chance to do their part, by making small changes everyday ... beautiful and healthy is how the earth would stay.

slumber.

organic cotton pillow sheets

ORGANIC SHEETS

meditation pillow

Recycled GLASS VASE

organic wool rug

RECYCLED PAPER AND JOURNAL

DREAMS

Bamboo BOOKCASE

SHERRY FLOWERS POEMS BIRDS HISTORY WATER THE SUN STORIES

COOK STORIES SHELLS MOUNTAINS LAKES WIND GARDEN RAIN

reclaimed wooden mirror

A room full of color, a place to dream, rather than television in bed you can read or tell stories instead. If its not too cold then turn down the heat and wake up each morning in an organic bed sheet.

feed

BULK FOODS GLASS JARS

organic and local fruits and vegetables

home-made apron

REUSABLE BAGS

reusable plates and utensils

Local Cook Book

reusable towels

organic

homemade breads

FRESH LOCAL EGGS

organic

biodegradeable soap

handmade clay bowls

EARTH

YOU

OUR COMMUNITY

PAPER

RECYCLE BINS

GLASS

reusable Lunch Box

RECYCLED PAPER

Compost bin

Find food that comes from a local farm and organic food that does the earth no harm. Grow fresh fruit and vegetables to eat and cook for family or friends you meet. Packaging gets thrown away so buy in bulk and save for another day. Reuse a bag at the grocery store, go to a farmers market and explore. Reduce buying plastic the reason would be, fish mistake it food and it stays in the sea.

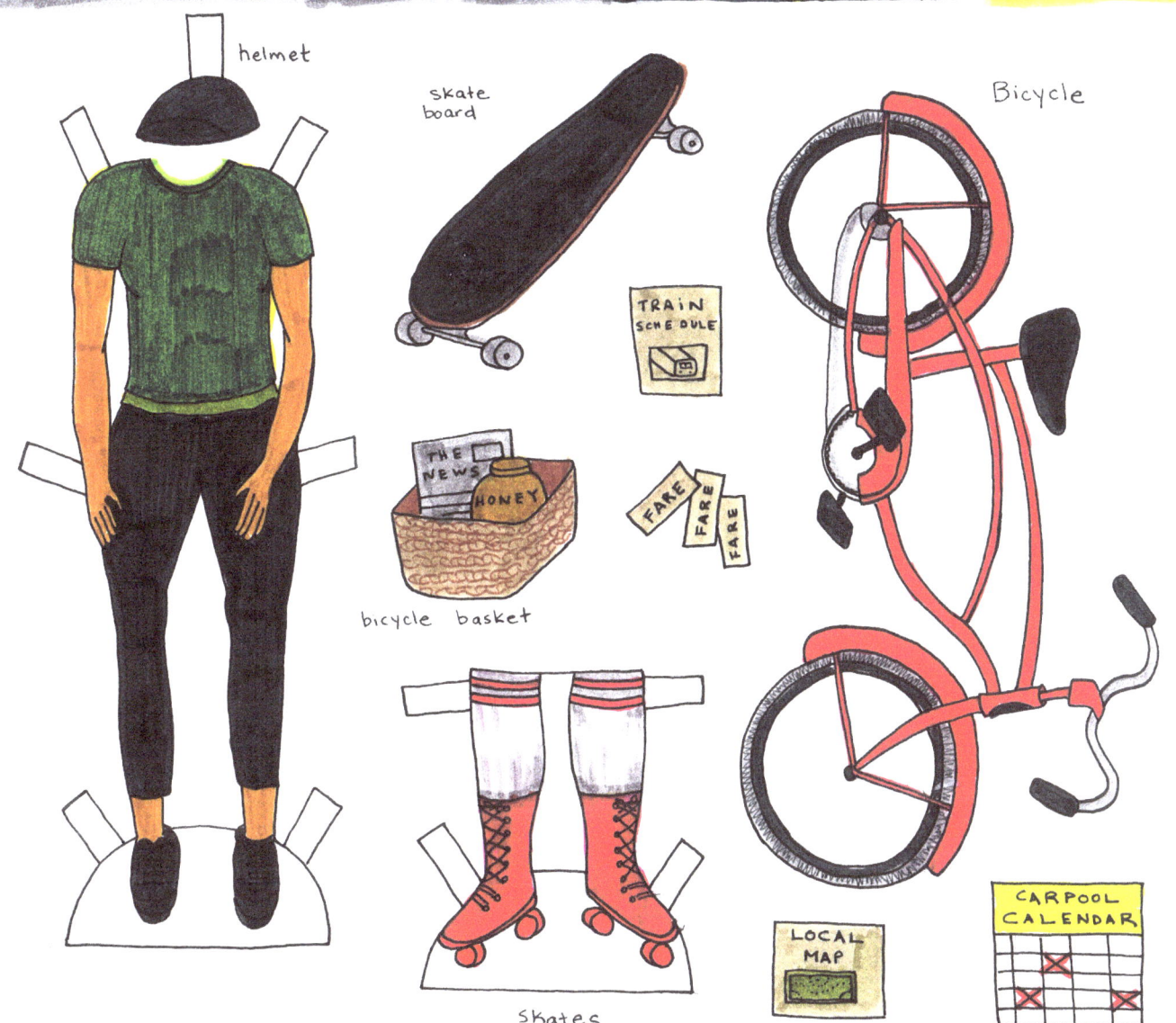

around

Green St.

helmet

skate board

Bicycle

TRAIN SCHEDULE

THE NEWS

HONEY

FARE FARE FARE

bicycle basket

LOCAL MAP

CARPOOL CALENDAR

Skates

So much joy you'll find in riding a bike, scooter or skate to any place you like. Walk or run where you need to go, you can go fast or take it slow. Cars that use gas pollute the air so travel by train and bus and share.

wash

vintage Kimono

sea sponges

Pumice stone

Sea salts

organic towels

reuse towels.

recycled toilet paper

low flow shower

Bucket to save and reuse water

HerBs

low flow sink

Dual Flush and Composting Toilet

biodegradeable.

Hand made Products

organic Products

recycled and natural Brushes

Make it a minute not up to an hour you waste too much water if its not a short shower. Have your water be heated by the sun, turn it off and don't let it run.

dwell

heat off

shade of paper and Bamboo

used chair

beeswax candles

recycled paper bowls

one earth

natural objects

lights off

aloe plant

reclaimed wood table

unplug

games

Sit near a window during the day, let enough light in to work and play. Turn off the light and things when not in use, in saving energy there is no excuse. Furniture can be used or found, there are many lovely things to go round. Fill the room with plants that clean the air and reuse items like an antique lamp or a fine lounge chair.

build

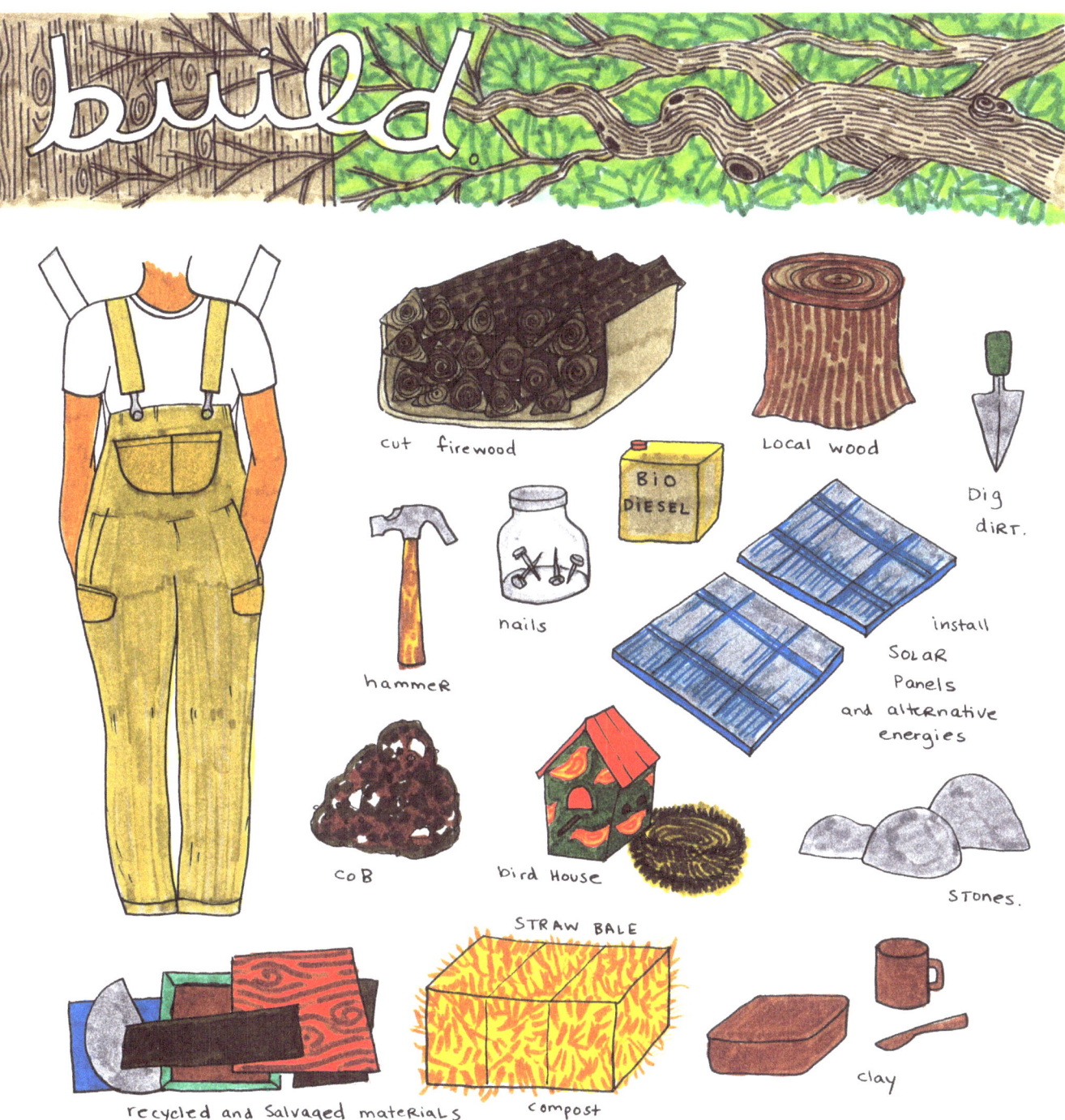

cut firewood

Local wood

BIO DIESEL

Dig diRt.

nails

hammeR

install SoLaR Panels and alternative energies

coB

bird House

STones.

STRAW BALE

recycled and Salvaged materiaLs

compost

clay

We build with trees that are cut down for wood; forests become empty where many trees stood. The wood can be used as fuel and trees provide oxygen, shade and the ground they cool. Climb up in their branches, look up and gaze, trees are special in so many ways. Plant more as they help the soil and air, once covering the land almost everywhere.

task

organic t-shirt

eco-friendly cleaning

Baking Soda

VINEGAR

Natural Brushes

reusable rags

Sustainable broom

Bamboo Dishrack

To keep a place tidy and clean, do not use chemicals that can be mean Biodegradable soap and water will do, with a little vinegar and baking soda too. Wash clothes on cold and hang them to dry, using the wind and the sun of the sky. Wash your dishes by hand to make them shine, let them air out and be ready to dine. Store your bottles, cans and paper away, put it out on the street on recycle day.

dig

aquaculture

flowers.

seeds

NATURAL PEST CONTROL

fruit trees.

rake

Tags.

PEAS

Hat and Sunscreen

Bags of compost and soil

shovel.

grey WATER

worms

compost

A compost bin is where extra food should be placed, rather than thrown in the garbage where it becomes waste. Add worms to the soil and grow what you eat, and sometimes in your compost choose not to add meat. Home to the birds and butterflies with wings, a garden is a place for all living things.

re-paint.

knit and crochet.

cut

thread.

resew

weave.

embroidery

embroidery

fabric scraps

found objects

natural dyeing

Sort the trash you can try to reuse, be creative and less you'll produce. Invite friends to a party where they all can partake, be amazed at how many interesting things you can make. You can sew your own clothes; re-make outfits that are old and let your fashion unfold. Don't throw them away but do a good deed, recycle your clothes or give them to people in need.

study

shapes of leaves

weather

lifecycles

Tidepools

Bird Calls

connections

rocks and minerals

animal tracks

Know the plants and animals that live in unity,
learn the names of every flower, bird and tree
in your community.

move

vintage
swim suit

home made
Mask

Make
Music!

Dance!

Drum

Snow shoe

frisbee

snow
board

guide
to
trails

play ball

jump rope

walking
stick

weights

sports

yoga
mat

Breathe and stretch when you arise, it clears your mind when you
exercise. It gets your heart to beat, finding so many ways to move
your feet. Go for a hike in the woods near your town and find the
nature that is all around. Come up with ideas and make games just for fun,
write and act in a play and invite a loved one. meet new people if you
have the chance, it takes no energy to get up and dance!

escape

Travel journal + books

Sun Screen

Binoculars

Games

Blankets

Compass

Hemp Backpack

Reusable Boxes

DREAM

Jar for water

eco friendly Surfboard

A journey can be anywhere, but to the land and people please show you care. There are so many cultures in the world to embrace, but you can also go to a local place. To the earth, air and water be kind, be good to people wherever you unwind.

connect

Through summer, fall, winter and spring, you are connected to everything. Patterns and cycles make up the great mystery, life and death is part of our natural history.

About the Author

Kirsten graduated in 2006 from the University of Vermont with a degree in Environmental Studies. Kirsten concentrated in education and ecological design with a graduating thesis researching the emerging green market and designed her own furniture, products and fashion made out of recycled and sustainable materials. Kirsten has traveled to Costa Rica, Ecuador and Peru studying conservation biology and sustainable development. After her undergraduate career she taught environmental education to inner city students in the redwood ecology of Northern California and worked in disadvantaged schools throughout New York City. While residing in Berkeley, California she partnered with a green design cooperative transforming an un-rented office supply store into an environmental community center and gallery. While residing in New York City she connected with a non-profit where she consulted to top fashion designers on sustainable textiles. Kirsten is a certified Permaculture teacher and designer, as well as a certified Hatha Yoga instructor. She dreams of soon having her own classroom in which to change the world.